T MacKeller

Hymns and a few Metrical Psalms

T MacKeller

Hymns and a few Metrical Psalms

ISBN/EAN: 9783744780827

Printed in Europe, USA, Canada, Australia, Japan

Cover: Foto ©Lupo / pixelio.de

More available books at **www.hansebooks.com**

HYMNS

AND A FEW

METRICAL PSALMS

BY

THOMAS MACKELLAR,
PH. D.

PHILADELPHIA:
PORTER & COATES.
1889.

FIRST EDITION.

SOME of the hymns in this volume were written before a busy life had passed its noontide: others, when the rays of the westering sun were falling slantwise. The latest were the outcome (as well as the alleviation) of times of anguish and bereavement.

A few of the earlier pieces have come into use in various hymnals. All that may be deemed fitting are at the service of the church.

April, 1883.

SECOND EDITION.

THE new hymns inserted in this edition are numbered from LXXII. to LXXXVI., and the additional psalms will be found on pages 193 to 206.

T. McK.

GERMANTOWN, PA.
May, 1889.

High and mighty God and Saviour!
On the earth thy will be done:
Hallowed be thy name forever,
Holy Father, Holy Son,
Holy Spirit!
Lord Jehovah!
Glory be to Thee alone.

First Lines.

	PAGE
After the darkness of the night	40
Again I take with hopeful heart	52
Alone with God to-day	34
A prisoner of the Lord	102
A refuge and a fortress	202
Art thou in thy spirit lowly	78
As children dwelling in their home	112
At Jesus' feet I take my place	124
At the door of mercy sighing	60
Bear the burden of the present	88
Before the silver cord be loosed	178
Be not anxious for the morrow	30
Be not disquieted, my soul!	22
Be still, my soul! be still	188
Blessed be thy name forever	58
Book of grace and book of glory!	156
Build up, O Lord, a rampart-wall	171
Cast thy burden on the Lord	132
Christ is risen! O the wonder!	139
Cold the bed and hard the pillow	183

	PAGE
Day is breaking in the sky	16
Day is waning into shadow	180
Draw nigh to the Holy	66
Far away the Saviour saw me	46
Far distant from my Father's house	92
Father! all is of thy giving	185
Father! in my life's young morning	150
Give ear unto my words, O Lord	195
Give me a foothold on the rock	126
Give me to know thy will, O God	44
Glory be to God on high!	138
Glory to God in the highest!	13
God has said it,—and his promise	82
Hallow'd day of sacred rest	68
I give myself to God	120
I have no hiding-place	38
I know not when the Lord will call	160
I lift my longing eyes	209
I long for God, the living God	98
In tearless anguish once I lay	74
In the hidden ways of life	114
In the midnight and the storm	116
In the vineyard of our Father	146
In vain the ways of Providence	54
I thank the Lord my Maker	152
I will extol thee every day	211
I would I were content to be	20

	PAGE
JEHOVAH reigns! Let earth rejoice	207
Jesus! when my soul is parting	62
LET all the people sing a psalm	96
Lord, take and lead me as a child	50
MY righteous God! O hear my call	193
My soul cries out to God	48
My soul is resting in God's peace	64
My soul! why sit forsaken	166
NEARER to thy heart of love	164
No tongue of man has ever told	108
O FATHER, for thy love!	174
O gracious Father! send us showers	72
O land of day, eternal day	136
O Lord, our Lord! in all the earth	197
O the agonizing prayer	130
O the blessedness of leaning	24
O the darkness, O the sorrow	176
Only in silence wait on God	205
Over the earth a stillness comes	94
REST and peace for Jesus' sake!	128
SITTING in the twilight musing	190
Some day the word will come to me	104
Sometimes, in quiet revery	134
THE billows round me rise and roll	70
The blessing of the Sabbath-day	106

	PAGE
The darkness of the night came down	80
The day is wearing fast away	76
The day of wrath, that certain day	142
The dusty paths of earth defile	118
The heavens declare the glory	199
The morning of the centuries	42
The morning stars were singing	148
The pathway to the mercy-seat	122
The sea before, the foe behind	162
There is a land immortal	84
There is light on my path	158
Though darkness turn the skies to night	26
'Tis but a looking unto Christ	168
'Tis well that thou, my God, shouldst be	86
Unseen by them, a glorious host	90
Upon the pillow of Thy love	18
Was Jesus tempted like as we	36
Watchers call'd to work for Jesus	32
What though the way be storm-begirt	28
When he waketh, when he sleepeth	100
Where could I go but unto thee	110
While some may run an easy pace	56
Who bids the wind to blow?	154

HYMNS.

I. . . . . 8, 5.

A multitude of the heavenly host praising God, and saying, Glory to God in the highest.—Luke ii. 13, 14.

I.

GLORY to God in the highest!
    The day of all days
    Awakens our praise,—
    The thrice-blessed morn
    When Jesus was born,—
The name that the church glorifieth:
      Glory to God!
      Glory to God!
Glory to God in the highest!

II.

Glory to God in the highest!
    Let heaven resound
    To its uttermost bound
    With anthems of praise
    Both now and always,

While seraph to seraph replieth,
    Glory to God!
    Glory to God!
Glory to God in the highest!

III.

Glory to God in the highest!
    Let earth, with its hills,
    Its valleys and rills,
    Re-echo his praise
    Both now and always,
While mountain to mountain-top crieth,
    Glory to God!
    Glory to God!
Glory to God in the highest!

IV.

Glory to God in the highest!
    His goodwill and peace
    To men will not cease:
    The church lifts her voice
    While angels rejoice,
And her song with the seraphim's vieth:
    Glory to God!
    Glory to God!
Glory to God in the highest!

V.

Glory to God in the highest!
　　The bountiful Lord,—
　　The Father, the Word,
　　The Spirit,—whose praise
　　Both now and always
On the wings of infinity flieth:
　　Glory to God!
　　Glory to God!
Glory to God in the highest!

1821.

II. . . . . 7's.

I laid me down and slept; I awaked; for the Lord sustained me.
Ps. iii. 5.

I.

DAY is breaking in the sky;
    Restful night has pass'd away:
Now I lift my early cry,
    Lead thy servant, Lord, to-day.

II.

Jesus, Master! forth I go,
    Taking up my 'custom'd task:
Teach me what I need to know,—
    Give me what I ought to ask.

III.

I see not the way before,
    But I go at thy command,
Entering gladly duty's door,
    Led by thy directing hand.

IV.

Take away my sin and guilt,
    Make me whiter than the snow:
Be my will just what Thou wilt,
    Asking not, Why is it so?

V.

May my soul, impell'd by love,
    Do whate'er thy Spirit saith,
That my life this day may prove,
    Through thy grace, the power of faith.

VI.

Glory to Thee evermore!
    Glory in the uttermost!
Heaven and earth thy name adore,
    Father, Son, and Holy Ghost.

1861.

III. . . . . C. M.

Yea, thou shalt lie down, and thy sleep shall be sweet.—Prov. iii. 24.

I.

UPON the pillow of Thy love
    My weary head I lay,
Assured that watchers from above
    Will round about me stay.

II.

The weanéd child, subdued and still,
    Sleeps on its mother's breast;
So I, submissive to thy will,
    Lean on thy strength for rest.

III.

The sighs, and tears, and agony
    That marr'd the hours of day,
Subside as tempests on the sea
    In silence die away.

IV.

The restful peace of answer'd prayer
    Is in my chasten'd heart:
My fears, my sorrows, and my care
    At thy command depart.

V.

O Lord, my God, my strength, my hope,
    In thee I find repose:
Vouchsafe my grateful eyes shall ope
    As softly as they close.

1821.

IV. . . . . C. M.

The way of man is not in himself: it is not in man that walketh to direct his steps.—Jer. x. 23.

I.

I WOULD I were content to be
    Just as my Lord shall will,
So I with cheerful constancy
    His purpose may fulfil.

II.

O may I be content to lay
    My hourly griefs and cares
Upon His arm that every day
    His children's burden bears:

III.

Nor proudly strive to carry part
    And leave to Him the rest,
So losing comfort of the heart
    And healing of the breast.

IV.

Though I should ask the Lord to show
    Some greater things to do,
May I be ever quick to go
    On humble errands too:

V.

To run in haste, or waiting stand,
    Content to go or stay,
While watching for his guiding hand
    To point the fitting way.

VI.

Whatever work the day shall bring,
    May I set Thee before,
And give to Thee, O Christ, my King,
    The glory evermore.

1881.

V. . . . . C. M.

It shall come to pass, that at evening time it shall be light.
Zech. xiv. 7.

I.

BE not disquieted, my soul!
   'Tis grace that moves the Power
Whose hand thy destinies control
   In every varying hour.

II.

When sorrows fall, he wraps the heart
   The closer in his love:
If here he takes away a part,
   He'll give thee all above.

III.

Why tremble when thy God shall lay
   A shadow on thy path?
Not e'en the dark, distressful day
   Portends a night of wrath.

IV.

The heavy clouds that, dark and dun,
    Thine upward pathway hide,
Shall blaze with glory when the sun
    Goes down at eventide.

V.

And light from God's abiding-place
    Shall fix the raptured eye,
The light of love in Jesus' face,
    To welcome thee on high.

1881.

VI. . . . . 8, 7, 4.

Cast thy burden upon the Lord, and he shall sustain thee.—Ps. lv. 22.

I.

O THE blessedness of leaning
    On a strength beyond thine own!
O the fulness of the meaning—
    O the sweetness of the tone—
        Cast thy burden
    On thy loving Lord alone.

II.

Often weary, yet contending,—
    Beaten down, again to rise,—
On his help alone depending,
    Looking up with trustful eyes,—
        Cast thy burden
    On the arm that built the skies.

III.

Take his easy yoke upon thee,
    Lowly be like him in heart:

Child, it was his love that won thee,
    Will he bid thee now depart
      With thy burden,
    When thy soul is full of smart?

IV.

Long ago the word was written,—
    Word to generations blest,—
Hear it, children sorely smitten,
    Hear it, ye of troubled breast,—
      Cast thy burden
    On the Lord: he'll give thee rest.

1881.

VII. . . . . C. M.

When my spirit was overwhelmed within me, then thou knewest my path.—Ps. cxlii. 3.

I.

Though darkness turn the skies to night,
    Though sorrows fill the air,
Nor moon nor stars my pathway light,
    Yet thou art with me there.

II.

I cannot see thee, but I know
    A stronger arm than mine
Upholds me in the time of woe,—
    Jesus! that arm is thine.

III.

Though words may fail when I would pray,
    And mute I lift my hands,
Thou hearest what I cannot say,
    And Gabriel near me stands.

IV.

A just God and a Saviour, thou
    Art full of love and grace:
Before thy majesty I bow
    With glad and trustful face.

V.

Thy sovereign grace gives sweet relief,
    Dispelling faithless gloom,
And the dark chamber of my grief
    Becomes a sunny room.

1851

VIII. . . . . C. M.

I will be with thee: I will not fail thee, nor forsake thee.
Josh. i. 5.

I.

WHAT though the way be storm-begirt,
    If Jesus lead thee on!
Thou shalt not suffer loss or hurt,
    Nor walk the path alone.

II.

Must thou do battle on the way?
    The arm of God is thine:
Does he unprop thine earthly stay?
    Upon that arm recline.

III.

Has he not pledged his word to save?
    Will he himself deny?
Will he not hold thee fast who gave
    His Son for thee to die?

IV.

The Father chasteneth whom he will,
    And some he wills to spare;
But not the less he loveth still
    The souls that meekly bear.

V.

O Lord, my timorous heart control;
    Forgive my doubt and sin:
Open the windows of my soul
    And let thy sunlight in.

1881.

IX. . . . . 8, 7.

Behold the birds of the heaven, that they sow not, neither do they reap, nor gather into barns; and your heavenly Father feedeth them. Be not therefore anxious for the morrow: for the morrow will be anxious for itself.—Matt. vi. 26, 34.

I.

BE not anxious for the morrow,
   Let the morrow have its cares:
Soul, be not forecasting sorrow;
   Grace is given to him who bears
Crosses that he does not borrow:
   God controls the unawares.

II.

Neither sowing, neither reaping,
   Gathering not to store away,
Birds are in the Father's keeping,—
   Cares he not when children pray?
Why then, faithless, sighing, weeping,
   Doubt him for the coming day?

III.

Lilies, toiling not nor spinning,
    Gleam in robes beyond compare:
Never king from time's beginning
    Had such glorious dress to wear:
Souls that cost his life in winning
    Christ will keep with loving care.

1881.

X. . . . . 8, 7, 4.

Blessed are those servants whom the Lord when he cometh shall find watching.—Luke xii. 37.

Watch ye, stand fast in the faith, quit you like men, be strong. 1 Cor. xvi. 13.

I.

WATCHERS call'd to work for Jesus,
    To the glory of his name,
In the field where'er he pleases
    Our glad services to claim,—
        Ever ready!
This our watchword and our aim.

II.

Watching for the revelation
    Of his glory and his grace,
When the power of his salvation
    Shall subdue earth's rebel race,—
        Always watching,
Always standing in our place.

III.

Watching for the coming morning,
    Resting in the Saviour's might,
Even now we see its dawning,
    See the shafts of heavenly light
        Pierce the darkness
That enwrapt the world in night.

IV.

Watching while our hands are doing;
    Loitering not on conquer'd ground;
Looking forward, still pursuing,
    While the golden trumpets sound;
        King eternal!
True to thee may we be found.

V.

Watching, hoping, toiling, praying,
    Till the victory is won,
May we then hear Jesus saying,
    "Toilers, rest! your work is done!"
        As we enter
Homes of rest beyond the sun.

1882.

XI. . . . . S. M.

Come, my people, enter thou into thy chambers, and shut thy doors about thee.—Isa. xxvi. 20.

I.

ALONE with God to-day,
   My soul subdued and still,
My thoughts ascend the upward way
   To Moses' lonely hill.

II.

From Nebo's utmost height
   Mine eyes look longingly
To the far distant land of light
   Beyond the glassy sea.

III.

I seem no stranger there,
   No traveller unknown:
For in that heavenly land so fair,
   My Lord is on the throne.

IV.

Among the company
  Who serve Him day and night,
Dear ones who walk'd on earth with me
  Walk now in robes of white.·

V.

Their work and waiting done,
  He call'd them of His grace;
Their higher service is begun
  Before the Saviour's face.

VI.

I cannot know while here
  The bliss of that sweet land;
But they have neither sin nor fear
  Who in His presence stand.

VII.

So I in gladness wait
  Before the Lord to-day,
While catching glimpses through the gate
  Of glory far away.

1881.

XII. . . . . C. M.

A high priest...that hath been in all points tempted like as we are, yet without sin.—Heb. vi. 15.

I.

WAS Jesus tempted like as we,
    The Holy One of God?
Were paths of pain and poverty
    By him, our Master, trod?

II.

Was there no place in all his earth
    To lay his head upon,
A King of more than royal birth,
    Yea, God's eternal Son?

III.

If thus the sinless Saviour fared,
    Can I, dare I repine,
When sorrow, want, and death he shared
    To make salvation mine!

IV.

O child redeem'd by his own blood,
    Why yield to anxious care?
Thou canst not sink beneath the flood
    When Christ is walking there.

V.

Think not thy Saviour does not see
    When Satan casts a dart:
No arrow ever wounded thee
    That did not pierce his heart.

VI.

The great High Priest is touch'd by all
    Thy weaknesses and woes;
And He, when grievous sorrows fall,
    Sufficient grace bestows.

1881.

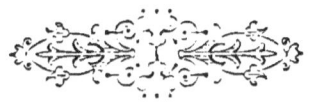

XIII. . . . . S. M.

O Lord, my strength, and my fortress, and my refuge in the day of affliction.—Jer. xvi. 19.

I.

I HAVE no hiding-place,
  No refuge from the blast,
But in the arms of Jesus' grace
  Around about me cast.

II.

Though I see not His hand,
  I feel its loving power:
And guardian angels near me stand
  In my distressful hour.

III.

I dare not look within,
  But heavenward turn my gaze;
And lest my grief become my sin,
  My tongue breaks out in praise.

IV.

Though tears mine eyes bedim,
  He dries the tears I shed;
And in my soul I sing a hymn,
  Content and comforted.

1880.

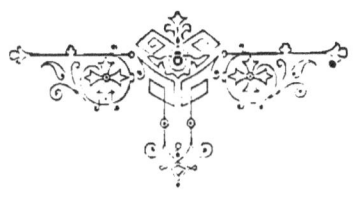

XIV. .... 8, 7, P.

Him that turneth the shadow of death into the morning.
Amos v. 8.

I.

AFTER the darkness of the night
    Light cometh in the morning;
After the winter and its blight
    Spring wakes in new adorning.

II.

After the sowing of the seed
    The harvest greets the reaper;
After the day of loving deed
    Soft rest enfolds the sleeper.

III.

After the tempest's course is run
    A calm pervades the waters;
After the work of life is done
    God calls his sons and daughters.

IV.

After the closing of the eye
    They wake with Christ in heaven;
After the final victory
    The crown of life is given.

1881.

XV. . . . . C. M.

So mightily grew the word of the Lord and prevailed.—Acts xix. 20.

I.

THE morning of the centuries
   Beheld a light arise,
That in their heavenly ministries
   Ne'er fell on angels' eyes.

II.

Through all the ancient days it seem'd
   A planet new-begun;
It grew in fulness till it beam'd
   A sun beyond the sun.

III.

When earth with clouds of sin was dark,
   It made an open way;
E'en where it glimmer'd as a spark,
   Some souls received the ray;

IV.

And they became the sons of God
    Amid a scoffing race;
While bloody was the way they trod,
    His peace lit up their face.

V.

They seal'd their constancy with blood;
    And where the martyrs died
A multitude arose and stood,
    And God was glorified.

VI.

That sun has never ceased to shine
    Upon the King's domain,
Pouring from heaven a light divine
    To make its pathway plain.

VII.

Till centuries shall be no more,
    Its light shall not grow dim;
And Christ's redeem'd on heaven's shore
    Shall sing redemption's hymn.

1881.

XVI. .... C. M.

Order my steps in thy word; and let not any iniquity have dominion over me.—Ps. cxix. 133.

I.

GIVE me to know thy will, O God,
    And may I see to-day
A light from heaven upon my road
    To clearly point the way:

II.

That I may know just what to do,
    And what to leave undone,
And be unto thy service true
    From dawn to setting sun:

III.

That I may speak the timely word,
    And timely silence keep,—
By passion's hasty words unstirr'd
    That cause the soul to weep:

IV.

That I may hold my thoughts in check,
    And every wild desire
That rises quick at pleasure's beck
    And flames into a fire:

V.

That I may kiss the needed rod,
    And patient bear the blow;
And say, 'Tis from the love of God;
    My Father wills it so.

VI.

Lord Jesus! from thy holy place
    The Spirit on me breathe:
Open the mantle of thy grace
    And keep my soul beneath.

1880.

XVII. .... 8, 7, 4.

But while he was yet afar off, his father saw him, and was moved with compassion.—Luke xv. 20.

I.

Far away the Saviour saw me,
  Lost and wandering in the wild:
By his love he sought to draw me,—
  Me unworthy and defiled,—
    As a father
Calls to him his erring child.

II.

I saw not the hand that beckon'd,
  I heard not his gracious call,
Till the joys on which I reckon'd,
  Worldly joys, had perish'd all;
    Then his mercy
Led me at his feet to fall.

III.

Jesus broke the chains that bound me,
    And his freeman I became:
Robes of grace he threw around me,
    Covering all my sin and shame:
        O how precious
    Is my great Deliverer's name!

IV.

Over all and bless'd forever,
    God on his eternal throne,
Who the bond of love can sever
    That unites to Christ his own?
        Lord Jehovah!
    Glory be to Thee alone.

                      1882.

XVIII. . . . . S. M.

O my God, my soul is cast down within me.—Ps. xlii. 6.

I.

MY soul cries out to God,
   Like children in the night,
Who fear some evil is abroad
   Because they see no light.

II.

There's darkness on the path,
   And pitfalls line the way,
Till fear of coming trouble hath
   An overpowering sway.

III.

It may be faith is weak;
   Perchance the heart is faint,
And in unutter'd words would speak
   Its longing, hungering plaint.

IV.

The duties left undone,
　　The follies unforgiven,
Rise up like clouds before the sun
　　And vail the face of heaven.

V.

So, desolate and lone,
　　The soul lifts up its cry
To Christ upon his gracious throne
　　Of majesty on high.

VI.

Lord, calm this restless mind,
　　From murmuring set me free,
And strength and comfort let me find
　　In earnest work for Thee.

1882.

XIX. . . . . C. M.

Therefore for thy name's sake lead me, and guide me.
Ps. xxxi. 3.

I.

LORD, take and lead me as a child
    That knows not how to go,
Alike when day is calm and mild
    And night's wild tempests blow.

II.

If grief and pain be mine to bear
    And sorrows bow my head,
Let not my heart sink in despair
    As though my Lord were dead.

III.

When I am weary, on the breast
    Of Him who died for me,
O let my laden spirit rest,
    From care and worry free.

IV.

When joy shall fill my earth and skies
    With a serenest calm,
Then may my thoughts to Thee arise
    In one continual psalm.

V.

When some sad brother turns to me
    In sore and heavy grief,
May I be quick in sympathy
    And quicker in relief.

VI

When some poor soul is sick of sin
    And seeks the way to God,
O make me wise that soul to win
    To take the heavenward road.

VII.

Lord, in the dark and in the light
    Still keep me in thy way,
A child whose hand is claspéd tight
    In thine by night and day.

1875.

XX. . . . . C. M.

Even there shall thy hand lead me, and thy right hand shall hold me.
Ps. cxxxix. 10.

I.

AGAIN I take with hopeful heart
   My life's allotted task:
To do it well the grace impart;
   This, Lord, I humbly ask.

II.

The day's perplexing mysteries
   I may not understand:
Be it enough my Father sees
   And holds them in his hand.

III.

My duty for the day is plain,—
   To go where God shall call,
Or, patient, hold the tangled skein
   While he unravels all.

IV.

I may not ask that no rough wind
    Upon my head shall blow,
Yet I may pray that I shall find
    Strength in the day of wo.

V.

The sun may shine through all the day,
    Or clouds may hide the sky,
But while God's love lights up my way
    I know his hand is nigh.

1882.

XXI. . . . . C. M.

Canst thou by searching find out God? canst thou find out the Almighty unto perfection.—Job xi. 7.

I.

IN vain the ways of Providence
   With anxious gaze I scan:
To find out God by human sense
   It is not given to man.

II.

Enough to know he cannot err
   When worlds his plans fulfil;
That not a blade of grass can stir
   But at its Maker's will.

III.

Enough to know that God is just,
   Yet with a father's heart;
Enough with loving faith to trust
   When earthly friends depart.

IV.

Enough to know he gave his Son
    My guilt and grief to bear,
That I, though by my sin undone,
    Might still his mercy share.

V.

Then let me nevermore repine
    Beneath the chastening stroke,
And be the willing spirit mine
    To wear the Saviour's yoke.

1882.

XXII. . . . . C. M.

Take thou part in suffering hardship, as a good soldier of Christ Jesus.—2 Tim. ii. 3.

I.

While some may run an easy pace
    With self-reliant boast,
The Lord e'er gives to those his grace
    Who seek and need it most.

II.

Beneath a quiet smile may lie
    A sorrow of the soul
That needs a daily victory
    To hold it in control.

III.

And they who bear the battle's brunt,
    And temper'd weapons wield,
Shall stand up grandly in the front
    And hold the conquer'd field.

IV.

God's rank and file, in battle line
  And truth's divine array,
Shall set their camp at day's decline
  Along the King's highway

V.

To that good land, by sense unknown,—
  That land whose name is Heaven,—
Where Christ doth gather all his own,
  And crowns of life are given.

1881.

XXIII. . . . . 8, 7, 4.

Our Lord Jesus Christ . . . the blessed and only Potentate, the King of kings, and Lord of lords; who only hath immortality, dwelling in light unapproachable, whom no man hath seen, nor can see: to whom be honour and power eternal. Amen.
1 Tim. vi. 14-16.

I.

BLESSED be thy name forever,
 Lord and Christ, eternal King!
While we live, our tongues shall never
 Fail thy glorious praise to sing,—
  While before Thee
 Thankful offerings we bring.

II.

In the fulness of the ages
 Thou as man didst come to earth:
Welcomed by the wisest sages,
 Israel saw not thy worth,—
  Yet what glory
 Heralded thy wondrous birth!

III.

Scorn'd by cruel men, they slew thee,
    Thou the Maker of them all!
Though so few were they that knew thee,
    Blest were they whom thou didst call,—
        Like their Master,
    By the hand of man to fall.

IV.

Throned in thy eternal glory,
    Myriads worship at thy feet:
May we bend with them before thee
    When our work shall be complete,—
        By thy Spirit
    Made for heavenly service meet.

1882.

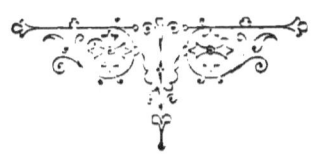

XXIV. .... 8, 7.

Come unto me, all ye that labour and are heavy laden, and I will give you rest.—Matt. xi. 28.

I.

At the door of mercy sighing
    With the burden of my sin,
Day and night my soul is crying,
    "Open, Lord, and let me in."
Waiting mid the darkness dreary,
    Stretching out my hands to Thee,
In the refuge for the weary
    Is there not a place for me?

II.

I have sought to earn thy favour,
    Caring not for toil or cost;
Yet I find not him my Saviour,
    Him who came to seek the lost.
Blessed Master! in thy pity
    Teach me what I ought to do,
So that in the holy city
    I may gain an entrance too.

III.

Hark! what sounds mine ear receiveth,
　　Sweet as songs of seraphim!
"He that in the Lord believeth
　　Life eternal hath in Him.
At the outer door why staying?
　　Nothing, soul! hast thou to pay:
Christ in love to thee is saying,
　　Weary child, come in to-day."

IV.

I knew not of Jesus' kindness!
　　I knew not of Jesus' grace!
O the blackness of the blindness
　　That could not behold his face!
I saw not the door was open,
　　Nor my Lord invite me in:
Grace is mine beyond my hoping,
　　Mercy mightier than my sin.

1871.

XXV. . . . . 8, 7, 4.

Fear not; I am the first and the last.... I am the Alpha and the Omega, the beginning and the end. I will give unto him that is athirst of the fountain of the water of life freely.
Rev. i. 17. xxi. 6.

I.

Jesus! when my soul is parting
　From this body frail and weak,
And the deathly dew is starting
　　Down this pale and wasted cheek,—
　　　Thine, my Saviour,
　Be the name I last shall speak.

II.

Jesus! when my memory wanders
　Far from loved ones at my side,
And in fitful dreaming ponders
　　Who are they that near me glide,—
　　　Last, my Saviour,
　Let my thoughts on thee abide.

III.

When the morn in all its glory
    Charms no more mine ear nor eye,
And the shadows closing o'er me
    Warn me of the time to die,—
      Last, my Saviour,
    Let me see thee standing by.

IV.

When my feet shall pass the river,
    And upon the farther shore
I shall walk, redeem'd for ever,
    Ne'er to sin—to die no more,—
      First, Lord Jesus!
    Let me see thee, and adore.

1848.

XXVI. . . . . C. M.

The peace of God, which passeth all understanding.—Phil. iv. 7.

I.

MY soul is resting in God's peace,
    Without a care or fear:
The tumults of my bosom cease,
    For Christ my Lord is here.

II.

The Spirit poureth from on high
    A sanctifying tide;
And, bathing in its stream of joy,
    My soul is satisfied.

III.

He driveth curious doubts away,
    He giveth childlike faith;
And so I take the yea or nay
    Just as my Saviour saith.

IV.

I have not other wish to be
    Than what my Lord ordains;
So what He knoweth best for me,
    That be my richest gains.

V.

A spirit meek and quieted
    Is better than a crown;
How rich the blessing on the head
    That Jesus sendeth down!

VI.

Here in his banquet-house I bide,
    His banner o'er me love,
And wait the coming eventide
    Of perfect peace above.

1870.

XXVII. . . . . 6, 5.

Draw nigh to God, and he will draw nigh to you.—James iv. 8.

I.

DRAW nigh to the Holy,
　　Bend low at His throne;
There, penitent, lowly,
　　Thy sinfulness own:
There, there, if thou yearnest
　　For pardon and rest,
There, fervent and earnest,
　　Prefer thy request.

II.

Confess thy backsliding,
　　Thy weakness and fears;
In Jesus confiding,
　　There pour out thy tears.
Think not He will scorn thee,
　　Though wretched thy case;
His hands will adorn thee
　　With garments of grace.

III.

More precious than treasure,
    More vast than the sea,
His love has no measure
    Nor limit to thee.
His easy yoke wearing,
    His pleasure abide;
In all thy cross-bearing,
    He'll walk by thy side.

IV.

Fear not the wild clangour
    That Satan may raise,
So God's righteous anger
    But pass from thy ways.
Whom Christ has forgiven
    Goes safely along,
Till in the high heaven
    He sings the new song.

V.

Then kneel to the Holy,
    Bend low at His throne;
There, penitent lowly,
    Thy sinfulness own:
There, soul! if thou yearnest
    For pardon and rest,
There, fervent and earnest,
    Prefer thy request.

1852.

XXVIII. . . . . 7's.

Remember the sabbath day, to keep it holy.—Ex. xx. 8.
And on the sabbath they rested according to the commandment.
Luke xxiii. 56.

I.

HALLOW'D day of sacred rest,
  Welcome, welcome to my breast:
All the week I've sigh'd to feel
Bliss thine hours alone reveal.

II.

Aching temples, throb no more;
Busy care, thy reign is o'er;
Troublous thoughts, flee far away
From this quiet resting-day.

III.

Faith's anticipations, rise!
Leap the barriers to the skies:
Upward soar, my soul, to Him
Loved by saints and seraphim.

IV.

Thankful praise, my lips, employ—
Utter all my rapturous joy:
Though o'er all things silence come,
Can a ransom'd soul be dumb?

V.

Priceless moments! rich and sweet:
Happy soul! at Jesus' feet,
Rest, oh rest!—when He is near,
Lovingly, hast thou a fear?

VI.

Master! lowly here I lie:
Look on me with gracious eye;
Lay the yoke of love on me,
Easy shall the burden be!

VII.

Saviour! may thy Sabbaths come
Laden with the hope of home:
On the day thy grace has given,
Fit me for thyself and heaven.

1842.

XXIX. . . . . C. M.

What time I am afraid, I will trust in thee.—Ps. lvi. 3.

I.

THE billows round me rise and roll,
    The storms of worldly care
Beat heavily upon my soul,
    And shroud me in despair:
Forsaken, comfortless, betray'd,
    With none to succour me,—
Father! what time I am afraid,
    Then will I trust in Thee!

II.

As feeble as the bruisèd reed,
    Infirm to will or do;
Oft working out the ungrateful deed
    'Twere better to eschew;
How were the sinking soul dismay'd
    But for this refuge-plea,—
Father, what time I am afraid,
    Then will I trust in Thee!

III.

When hope is faint, and faith is weak,
    And fears the bosom fill,
And I a strong assurance seek
    That thou art gracious still;
I rest upon thy promise-word,
    To thine own truth I flee:
Father, what time I am afraid,
    Then will I trust in Thee!

IV.

When saintly paleness marks my face,
    And dimness fills mine eye,
And, hoping only in thy grace,
    I bow my head to die;
If, entering in the vale of shade,
    Nor sun nor star I see,
Father, what time I am afraid,
    Then will I trust in Thee!

1853.

XXX. . . . . C. M.

He prayed again; and the heaven gave rain, and the earth brought forth her fruit.—James v. 18.

I.

O GRACIOUS Father! send us showers,
   The gentle showers of rain,
To cheer the corn, the grass, the flowers,
   On mountain-side and plain.

II.

Command the pregnant clouds to rise
   And vail the fiery sun,
While from the fountains of the skies
   The streams of blessing run.

III.

O gracious Father! send us showers;
   The cattle mutely stand
Amid the scorch'd and wither'd bowers;
   Have mercy on our land!

IV.

The spider's web is on the mead,
    The worm consumes the leaf;
And all thy works before Thee plead
    The silent plea of grief.

V.

O gracious Father! send us showers;
    Regard our earnest cries;
But meek submission still be ours
    While our petitions rise.

VI.

To Thee each living thing looks up;
    Thou mad'st—thou'lt not destroy:
The overflow of mercy's cup
    Shall wake creation's joy.

1852.

XXXI. . . . . L. M.

For so he giveth his beloved sleep.—Ps. cxxvii. 2.

I.

IN tearless anguish once I lay,
    And every tender string of life
Was rudely smitten by disease,
    And nature quiver'd in the strife.

II.

To God I look'd for help the while
    The lingering moments seem'd to creep,
These words of grace broke on my mind,
    "He giveth his belovèd sleep."

III.

A gentle peace, like evening winds
    In summer from the ocean's breast,
Moved o'er my sighing, sinking soul,
    And soothed my murmurings all to rest;

IV.

And through that weary night of pain,
　　When it were manliness to weep,
My soul was comforted by this,
　　"He giveth his belovèd sleep."

V.

When prison'd long, my soul would fain
　　Leap through her fragile walls and flee,
But on the unmeasured life beyond
　　She, halting, gazes tremblingly;

VI.

Then may I simply trust in Him
　　Whose arms his feeblest follower keep,
And close mine eyes, and say, in death,
　　"He giveth his belovèd sleep!"

1842.

XXXII. . . . . C. M.

Or ever the silver cord be loosed, or the golden bowl be broken.
Eccl. xii. 6.

I.

THE day is wearing fast away,
　　The night is coming on,
To end the earthly pilgrimage
　　Begun at being's dawn.

II.

The voice of earthly friends no more
　　Within my soul can reach;
Another world hath round me grown,
　　Earth hath another speech.

III.

Now fain am I to go when He
　　Who sent me here shall call:
I wait his gentle breath to cause
　　The ancient tree to fall.

IV.

I long to lay my burden down,
    And in earth's bosom rest
As calmly as an infant sleeps
    Upon its mother's breast.

V.

Welcome, approaching shades of even,
    By idling triflers shunn'd!
I see the immortal life of heaven,
    And Christ, my God, beyond!

1840.

XXXIII. . . . .8, 7, 4.

Peter was grieved because he said unto him the third time, Lovest thou me? And he said unto him, Lord, thou knowest all things; thou knowest that I love thee.—John xxi. 17.

I.

Art thou in thy spirit lowly,
   Like the Man of Nazareth?
Art thou seeking to be wholly
     Join'd to him, come life, come death?
        Lov'st thou Jesus
     More than thine own vital breath?

II.

Is thy bosom full of sorrow?
   Is a cloud upon thy way?
Why the worldling's burden borrow?
     Child of grace and promise, say!
        Lov'st thou Jesus?
     Joy should be thy guest to-day.

III.

Hath God made all men to praise thee?
    Or art thou to fame unknown?
Only seek that he should raise thee
    Up to an immortal throne.
        Lov'st thou Jesus?
    He'll provide for all his own.

IV.

Care not thou how low thy station,
    If thy God hath chosen thee
Heir of glory and salvation
    Now and evermore to be!
        Lov'st thou Jesus?
    Life is thine eternally.

1870.

XXXIV. . . . . C. M.

Then he arose, and rebuked the winds and the sea; and there was a great calm.—Matt. viii. 26.

I.

THE darkness of the night came down
   And on my soul it lay,
As if my righteous Maker's frown
   Were gathering round my way.

II.

As lonely as if I alone
   In all the earth were left,—
As helpless as an infant-one
   Of mother's care bereft,—

III.

How swift and sure had been my doom
   Had Christ forgotten me!
A voice arose amid the gloom,
   "Thy Saviour loveth thee!"

IV.

Immediately there was a calm,
    A calm without, within;
For Jesus wrote upon my palm
    Full pardon of my sin.

V.

The inward tempests rage no more,
    The spirit's sorrows cease,
When Jesus stands upon the shore,
    And gently whispers, "Peace!"

1846.

XXXV. . . . . 8, 7, 4.

I shall give thee the heathen for thine inheritance, and the uttermost parts of the earth for thy possession.—Ps. ii. 8.

I.

GOD has said it,—and his promise
  Stands as firmly as his throne,—
Earth shall be a sure possession
  Granted to his Son alone;
    And the heathen
  Jesus' gracious reign shall own.

II.

Where a soul in guilt is lying,
  There his gospel shall be sent;
Life and grace for wretches dying,
  Balm for bosoms sad and rent:
    News of mercy,
  All shall hear the call, Repent!

III.

Thou the Lord of all creation,
    Every living soul is thine:
May the grace of thy salvation
      On the lands of darkness shine:
        Holy Spirit!
    To thyself the world incline.

IV.

Words of precious promise, spoken
    In thy faithfulness and love,
Never, never can be broken
      While thou reignest King above:
        Let thy mercies
    Thy abounding goodness prove.

1841.

XXXVI. .... 7, 6.

Yea, though I walk through the valley of the shadow of death, I will fear no evil: for thou art with me; thy rod and thy staff they comfort me.—Ps. xxiii. 4.

I.

THERE is a land immortal,
    The beautiful of lands;
Beside its ancient portal
    A sentry grimly stands:
He only can undo it,
    And open wide the door;
And mortals who pass through it
    Are mortal nevermore.

II.

That glorious land is Heaven,
    And Death the sentry grim:
The Lord thereof has given
    The opening keys to him;
And ransom'd spirits, sighing
    And sorrowful for sin,
Pass through the gate in dying,
    And freely enter in.

III.

Though dark and drear the passage
    That leads unto the gate,
Yet grace attends the message
    To souls that watch and wait;
And at the time appointed
    A messenger comes down,
And guides the Lord's anointed
    From cross to glory's crown.

IV.

Their sighs are lost in singing;
    They're blessed in their tears:
Their journey heavenward winging,
    They leave on earth their fears.
Death like an angel seeming,
    "We welcome thee!" they cry:
Their eyes with glory gleaming,
    'Tis life for them to die.

1845.

XXXVII. . . . . L. M.

It is God which worketh in you both to will and to work, for his good pleasure.—Phil. ii. 13.

I.

'TIS well that thou, my God, shouldst be
　The master of my destiny;
For were my lot placed in my hand,
Where should my sure salvation stand?

II.

Beset around with wily snares,
And cumber'd with uncounted cares,
What arm but thine alone can hold
My soul within thy saving fold?

III.

The things of sense allure mine eyes,
And sudden sins my soul surprise:
Were I no more thy grace to share,
Then naught were left me but despair.

IV.

I know that I am safe with thee;
Then in thy hands my portion be:
I cannot fear what may betide
When on thyself my hopes abide.

V.

Let sinless ones on merit stand,
I seek for mercy at thy hand:
No other way of help I see,
Thy grace in Christ must work for me.

VI.

A wretch were I to lean upon
The works my erring hands have done:
I stand a suppliant, with the plea,
Atoning blood was shed for me.

VII.

O let thy Spirit day by day
Uphold me in the upward way:
Enough for me that thou wilt keep
The feeblest of thy chosen sheep.

1846.

XXXVIII. . . . . 8, 7.

Let not your heart be troubled: ye believe in God, believe also in me.
John xiv. 1.

I.

BEAR the burden of the present,
    Let the morrow bear its own;
If the morning sky be pleasant,
    Why the coming night bemoan?

II.

If the darken'd heavens lower,
    Wrap thy cloak around thy form;
Though the tempest rise in power,
    God is mightier than the storm.

III.

Steadfast faith and hope unshaken
    Animate the trusting breast;
Step by step the journey's taken
    Nearer to the land of rest.

IV.

All unseen, the Master walketh
    By the toiling servant's side:
Comfortable words he talketh,
    While his hands uphold and guide.

V.

Grief, nor pain, nor any sorrow
    Rends thy breast to him unknown;
He to-day and He to-morrow
    Grace sufficient gives his own.

VI.

Holy strivings nerve and strengthen,
    Long endurance wins the crown:
When the evening shadows lengthen,
    Thou shalt lay the burden down.

1852.

XXXIX. . . . . C. M.

A host compassed the city both with horses and chariots.
2 Kings vi. 15.

I.

UNSEEN by them, a glorious host
   About God's people stand:
The heavenly watchers hold the post
   At his supreme command.

II.

There is no child of God too high
   To need their constant care,
And none too deep in poverty
   Their daily help to share.

III.

When loved ones go, and earth is lone,
   As if no friend were near,
Then unseen angels from the throne
   Bring helpful words of cheer.

IV.

The sun of hope breaks through our gloom,
　　And wondering whence it came,
We start, like Mary at the tomb
　　When Jesus call'd her name.

V.

Say, who can snatch from God away
　　His blood-redeeméd ones?
And who the heavenward course can stay
　　Of God Almighty's sons?

1882.

XL. . . . . C. M.

The ransomed of the Lord...shall come to Zion with songs.
Isa. xxxv. 10.

I.

FAR distant from my Father's house
    I would no longer stay;
But gird my soul and hasten on,
    And sing upon the way!

II.

The skies are dark, the thunders roll,
    And lightnings round me play;
Let me but feel my Saviour near,
    I'll sing upon the way!

III.

The night is long and drear, I cry;
    O when will come the day?
I see the morning-star arise,
    And sing upon the way!

IV.

When care and sickness bow my frame,
    And all my powers decay,
I'll ask Him for His promised grace,
    And sing upon the way!

V.

He'll not forsake me when I'm old,
    And weak, and blind, and gray;
I'll lean upon his faithfulness,
    And sing upon the way!

VI.

When angels bear me home to heaven,
    Disrobed of mortal clay,
I'll enter in the pearly gates,
    And sing upon the way!

1842.

XLI......8, 7, P.

The Lord is good to all; and his tender mercies are over all his works.—Ps. cxlv. 9.

I.

OVER the earth a stillness comes,
    The eventide is falling:
Lord, bless all dwellers in their homes
    Who on thy name are calling.

II.

Thy blessing on the toiler rest;
    The over-worn and weary;
The dying, and the comfortless
    To whom the earth is dreary.

III.

Thy blessing on the child to-night;
    Thy blessing on the hoary;
The maiden clad in beauty bright,
    The young man in his glory.

IV.

Thy blessing on my fellow-race,
    Of every clime and nation:
May they partake thy saving grace,
    O Giver of salvation.

V.

If any man have wrought me wrong,
    Still blessings be upon him:
May I in love to him be strong,
    Till charity have won him.

VI.

Thy blessings on me, from of old,
    My God! I cannot number:
I wrap me in their ample fold,
    And sink in trustful slumber.

1853.

XLII. . . . . L. M.

Take a psalm, and bring hither the timbrel, the pleasant harp with the psaltery.—Ps. lxxxi. 2.

I.

LET all the people sing a psalm,
    A stately psalm of solemn praise,
While sitting in the holy calm,
    The calm befitting Sabbath days.

II.

Come, chant the words King David sang
    When heavenly airs around him swept,
And Zion's tents with music rang,
    While holy day the singers kept.

III.

The King of glory on his throne,
    The Ancient of eternal days,
The infinite and triune One,
    Immortal strains become his praise.

IV.

Let all the tribes of Adam's race,
    With thankful voice and lifted palms,
E'er magnify his truth and grace
    And laud him in the ancient psalms.

1868.

XLIII. . . . . C. M.

If any man thirst, let him come unto me, and drink.—John vii. 37.

I.

I LONG for God, the living God;
    I hunger for his grace:
I long to see as I have seen
    My heavenly Saviour's face.

II.

The earth has not a home for me
    Where I would always stay:
O let me take my pilgrim-staff
    And speed my upward way.

III.

I would not be afraid to live,
    Nor yet afraid to die;
Nor wish to end my working days,
    Or make them faster fly.

IV.

But I would hide myself beneath
    Jehovah's sheltering wing,
And wait till his appointed hour
    Shall life immortal bring.

V.

Lord, may I learn to work or wait,
    Just as thy word is given,—
Not loitering idly at the gate
    That opens into heaven.

1866.

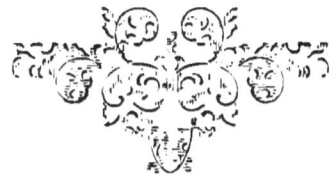

XLIV. . . . . 8, 7.

Whom the Lord loveth he chasteneth, and scourgeth every son whom he receiveth.—Heb. xii. 6.

I.

WHEN he waketh, when he sleepeth,
    When he toileth in the day,
Him the Father safely keepeth
    Who makes Christ his only stay.

II.

If he wanders, God will chasten
    Him with many stripes or few,
Till his erring footsteps hasten
    To the mercy-seat anew.

III.

If he meekly beareth crosses,
    And his eyes yet look to heaven,
God will turn to gain his losses,
    Yea, to him will much be given.

IV.

Daily he will find a token
    That his Lord loves to the end:
When the golden bowl is broken,
    Up to him shall he ascend.

V.

No more sin and no more sorrow,
    No more bitter tears to shed;
Heaven will have no sad to-morrow,
    But eternal day instead.

1882.

XLV. . . . . S. M.

The Lord will strengthen him upon the bed of languishing.
Ps. xli. 3.

I.

A PRISONER of the Lord,
    Awaiting his commands,
My prison-house is amply stored
    With bounties from his hands.

II.

He makes my pillow soft
    While prostrate, weak, and sore,
And ministering angels oft
    Enter my chamber-door.

III.

Sweet love in every tone
    Is whisper'd round my bed:
I know that none will give a stone
    Instead of strengthening bread.

IV.

No fears my soul alarm;
    My pains shall pass away:
Christ puts his everlasting arm
    Beneath me all the day.

V.

How can I be cast down?
    Why wrap myself in gloom,
And wear a care-begotten frown,
    When Christ is in the room?

VI.

God's strokes are not in wrath:
    The fruits that feed the soul
Bestrew the strait and narrow path
    Unto the heavenly goal.

1882.

XLVI. . . . . L. M.

Secretly saying, The Master is here, and calleth thee.—John xi. 28.

I.

SOME day the word will come to me,
　Arise; the Master calls for thee.
May I be ready then to go,
Saying, Lord Jesus! even so.

II.

Will work I've purposed in my thought
Be to my Master's pleasure wrought?
And will more talents then be won,
So that the Lord may say, Well done?

III.

Will tears be shed upon my bier
By some I've help'd to comfort here?
Will seed I've sown some fruitage bear
Too late for me the joy to share?

IV.

Shall I on Jordan's farther side
Find some redeem'd and glorified
To whom I pointed out the road
Leading to that divine abode?

V.

I cannot answer Yea or Nay:
This only, Master, can I say:
If I've done aught to honour thee,
It was thy grace that wrought through me.

VI.

O blessed Lord, in me abide
When I pass over Jordan's tide,
That I with my last trembling breath
May glorify thy name in death.

1882.

XLVII. . . . . C. M.

On that day, the first day of the week, ... Jesus came and stood in the midst.—John xx. 19.

I.

THE blessing of the Sabbath-day
　　Again our spirit cheers,
And heaven seems not so far away
　　That on our listening ears

II.

Some sounds of music may not fall
　　Struck on angelic lyres,
Some anthems to the Lord, by all
　　The high celestial choirs.

III.

Let our lips, too, break forth in praise
　　To thee, O King of heaven,
For this the chiefest of the days,
　　The holiest of the seven.

IV.

O Thou who on this day didst rise
    Omnipotent above,
Reveal to our expectant eyes
    New glimpses of thy love.

V.

Come, Holy Comforter, and show
    Thy gracious sovereign power,
That we may more like Jesus grow
    In this accepted hour.

VI.

As on the day of Pentecost,
    Visit thy church again,
That earth may join the heavenly host
    In praising Thee. Amen.

1882.

XLVIII. . . . . C. M.

Things which eye saw not, and ear heard not, and which entered not into the heart of man.—1 Cor. ii. 9.

I.

NO tongue of man has ever told
    God's everlasting love;
No heart has known the manifold
    Delights prepared above.

II.

Eye has not seen, ear has not heard
    These great and marvellous things,
Laid up for all who trust his word,
    For poor as well as kings.

III.

God's children daily something learn
    While training in his schools:
More clearly do their minds discern
    How gracious are his rules:

IV.

Yet little can they apprehend
    What God has still in store;
For that which has no bound nor end
    They cannot reckon o'er.

V.

Glory to thee, eternal King!
    Invisible, yet known
To loving souls who daily bring
    Faith's offering to thy throne.

1882.

XLIX. . . . . C. M.

Jesus said therefore unto the twelve, Would ye also go away?
John vi. 67.

I.

WHERE could I go but unto thee,
    O man of Nazareth?
Thy blood was shed on Calvary
    To give me life for death!

II.

To whom, my Lord, but unto thee,
    O Son of God most high,
When angels bend with reverent knee
    Before thy majesty?

III.

Where can I go but unto thee,
    The only refuge-tower
Impregnable, where I can flee
    In sore temptation's hour?

IV.

To whom need I go but to thee?
    Thou art the utmost sum
Of every soul's necessity;—
    And therefore, Lord, I come.

V.

O Lamb of God, who cam'st to take
    The sin of man away,
Fast hold me for thy mercy's sake,
    And I shall never stray.

1882.

L. . . . . C. M.

For as often as ye eat this bread, and drink the cup, ye proclaim the Lord's death till he come.—1 Cor. xi. 26.

I.

As children dwelling in their home
    By right of grace divine,
Unto thy table, Lord, we come
    To take of bread and wine.

II.

The bread shows forth thy body slain,
    The wine thy blood out-pour'd:
To take away our sin and stain
    Cost thy dear life, O Lord.

III.

O may the Holy Ghost descend
    With blessing from above,
That grateful praise may now ascend
    For thine amazing love.

IV.

Abide with us this holy day
    And fill us with thy peace,
And while we gladly praise and pray,
    Lord, make our faith increase.

V.

Sit with us at the blessed feast,
    As in the day of old,
Our high and sovereign Saviour-Priest,
    Thy glory to behold.

1882.

LI. . . . . 7's.

There was at the table reclining in Jesus' bosom one of his disciples, whom Jesus loved.—John xiii. 23.

I.

IN the hidden ways of life
   God's belovéd may be found,
Shut in from the things of strife,
   Hedged with mercies all around.

II.

Born of God they know not when,
   Single is the faith they hold,
Prying not with curious ken
   Into what has not been told.

III.

Like the saint of Patmos isle,
   In them love has potent sway,
Israelites who have no guile,
   Passing on their heavenward way:

IV.

By the loving, kindly deed,
    By the strengthening word of cheer,
By the helpful hand in need,
    Glorifying Jesus here.

V.

Pointing out the path to heaven,
    Winning souls is their reward:
When the welcome-call is given,
    Dying, they wake in the Lord.

1882.

LII. . . . . 7's.

After ye were enlightened, ye endured a great conflict of sufferings.
Heb. x. 32.

I.

IN the midnight and the storm
   Some of God's beloved must go;
Not for them the valleys warm,
   But the hills of crag and snow.

II.

In the darkness call'd to stand,
   Fighting with a foe unseen,
Friend nor lover at their hand,
   Strongly on their Lord they lean.

III.

Chasten'd sore, bereaved, and lone,
   They with steadfast faith look up,
Seeking, low before his throne,
   Grace to take the bitter cup.

IV.

Not the less beloved are they,
    Heirs with Christ, who suffer loss:
They shall find, some coming day,
    Why 'twas theirs to bear the cross.

V.

Some the fight of faith must share;
    Some endure the tempter's blows;
Testimony they must bear
    Christ is mightier than his foes.

VI.

As they lay their weapons by,
    Conquerors in the final strife,
Glory be to God! they cry,
    Entering into restful life.

1882.

LIII. . . . . C. M.

Jesus answered him, If I wash thee not, thou hast no part with me.
John xiii. 8.

I.

THE dusty paths of earth defile
   My sandals through the day;
And vexing cares my soul beguile
   While toiling on the way.

II.

How oft I lose the gracious sense
   Of nearness unto Thee!
How oft forget the providence
   That orders life for me!

III.

The daily good that I would do
   Is often unbegun;
And evil I would fain eschew
   My heedless hands have done.

IV.

At eventime, unsatisfied,
    I call the day to mind;
And by thy righteous standard tried,
    Shortcomings do I find.

V.

O Thou who, in thy graciousness,
    Didst wash thy servants' feet,
Thy travel-stain'd disciple bless
    Before thy mercy-seat.

VI.

The robe of works that I have worn
    Is scanty for my needs:
Give me the robe of thy new-born,—
    Of faith and holy deeds.

1882.

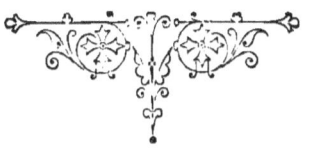

LIV..... S. M.

Ye are not your own; for ye were bought with a price.
1 Cor. vi. 19, 20.

I.

I GIVE myself to God,
  My life, my soul, my all:
He knows the devious paths I've trod,
  In mercy's hand I fall.

II.

My sins I cannot count,
  Nor sum his favours up:
I humbly kneel at mercy's fount
  And take salvation's cup.

III.

I proffer but his own;
  And may the Master take
The gift I lay before his throne,
  For my Redeemer's sake.

IV.

I give myself to God,
  For evermore to hold:
I pass beneath the Shepherd's rod
  To bide within his fold.

1882.

LV.....C. M.

And him that cometh to me I will in no wise cast out.—John vi. 37.

I.

THE pathway to the mercy-seat
  Is found of all who will;
And they who kneel at Jesus' feet
  Find him a Saviour still.

II.

As, when upon the earth he trod,
  None empty went away
Who sought his blessing as their God,
  So we to him may pray.

III.

The child unto his parent runs
  For comfort and relief:
So may the Lord's redeeméd ones
  Go to him with their grief.

IV.

Yea, even in the busiest hour
    Unspoken prayer may rise,
And blessings in a gracious shower
    Fall on us from the skies.

V.

We bless and magnify thy name,
    O Thou that answerest prayer:
In every age thou art the same
    To all who trust thy care.

1882.

LVI. . . . . C. M.

As many as touched him were made whole.—Mark vi. 56.

I.

At Jesus' feet I take my place:
    I touch his garment's hem:
A helpless child in need of grace
    My Lord will not condemn.

II.

I have no hope but in his love;
    His promise is my plea:
I give myself to Him who strove
    E'en unto death for me.

III.

I only ask that I may know
    What he would have me do,
That my obedient life may show
    The grace that bears me through.

IV.

I've nothing, Lord, to offer thee
    But this weak heart of mine:
O take it, Lord, and let it be
    Thine own, for ever thine.

1882.

LVII. . . . . C. M.

And the rock was Christ.—1 Cor. x. 4.

I.

GIVE me a foothold on the rock:
    The billows round me roll:
Let not their wild, impetuous shock
    O'erwhelm my trembling soul.
O Thou that walkest on the wave,
    Thou Ruler of the sea,
Stretch forth thy mighty arm to save
    The soul that calls on thee.

II.

Give me a foothold on the rock,
    O Saviour of the lost!
The world and sin my struggles mock,
    And I am tempest-tost.
I strive to reach an anchoring place:
    My God, give me a stay;
Extend to me thy hand of grace,
    Lest I be cast away.

III.

Give me a foothold on the rock,
    Till voices 'yond the sea,
Like evening chimings of the clock,
    Bid welcome home to me.
The day of toil and watching o'er,
    The night of sorrow past,
I step upon the eternal shore,
    And rest in peace at last.

1882.

LVIII. .... 7's.

The Lord lift up his countenance upon thee, and give thee peace.
Num. vi. 26.

I.

REST and peace for Jesus' sake!
   O my Father, hear my cry;
Heal my bosom's bitter ache,
   While before thy feet I lie.

II.

I have loved and I have lost
   Those whom I had prized too well:
O'er my threshold sorrow cross'd
   When the cherish'd idols fell.

III.

I forgot that they were lent,
   And I claim'd them as my own,
Till the message from thee sent
   Took them up before thy throne.

IV.

Speak the word of peace to me;
    Pardon thy forgetful child:
Let me find my rest in thee,
    Comforted and reconciled:

V.

Comforted, that loving eyes
    Shone so long within my home:
Reconciled, that to the skies
    Thou didst bid the loved ones come.

VI.

Rest and peace for Jesus' sake!
    Father, at thy feet I kneel:
Bruiséd reeds thou wilt not break,
    Thou the broken heart wilt heal.

1882.

LIX.... 7's.

Then cometh Jesus with them unto a place called Gethsemane.
Matt. xxvi. 36.

I.

O THE agonizing prayer
   Rising on the midnight air!
"Let this cup pass from thy Son:
Not my will, but thine be done!"
     Jesus in Gethsemane!

II.

O the tears and bloody sweat
Falling fast on Olivet!
In thy lonely agony,
Shedding crimson tears for me,
     Jesus in Gethsemane!

III.

O what wrath of earth and hell
On thy head unpitying fell,
When thy passion-time began,
Bearer of the sin of man,
     Jesus in Gethsemane!

IV.

Sorrow none had ever known
Came upon thy soul alone:
While its billows o'er thee swept,
Near at hand thy followers slept,
    Jesus in Gethsemane!

V.

Waken me from sinful sleep:
Faithful, loving, make me keep,
Watching every hour with thee
Who didst agonize for me,
    Jesus in Gethsemane!

VI.

Crimson'd once, but beauteous now,
O what glory crowns thy brow!
All the world shall bend the knee,
Lord triumphant! unto thee,
    Conqueror in Gethsemane!

1883.

LX. .... 7's.

Casting all your anxiety upon him, because he careth for you.
1 Peter v. 7.

I.

CAST thy burden on the Lord!
 Is this message meant for me?
May I take him at his word,
 And will he my helper be?

II.

In my daily household care,
 In the business of the day,
Will the Lord the burden bear
 Or his strength upon me lay?

III.

When the evil one shall cast
 Tempting baits to snare my soul,
Or shall taunt me with the past,
 Will the Lord his power control?

IV.

When the bitterness of grief
    Shall upon my bosom prey,
Will he give me swift relief?
    Will he take the pain away?

V.

When the parting hour is near;
    Will his everlasting love
Conquer every doubt and fear
    And the sting of death remove?

VI.

'Tis the promise of the Lord,
    Meant for me on every day:
Heaven and earth may fail,—his word
    Never once shall pass away.

1882.

LXI. . . . . C. M.

Behold, my servants shall sing for joy of heart.—Isa. lxv. 1.

I.

SOMETIMES, in quiet revery,
    When day is growing dim,
The heart is singing silently
    A sweet unwritten hymn.

II.

The strains are not to measure wrought
    By cunning of the mind,
But seem like hymnings angels brought
    From heaven, and left behind.

III.

The misty hills of bygone grief,
    Once dark to look upon,
Stand out like blessings in relief
    Against the setting sun.

IV.

The rain may fall, the wind may blow,
    The soul unhinder'd sings,
While, like the bird 'neath sheltering bough,
    She sits with folded wings,—

V.

A brief and pleasant resting space,
    A glance at Beulah land,
Before she girds herself apace
    For work that waits the hand.

VI.

Then, giving thanks to Him who pour'd
    Refreshment in her cup,
She hears the calling of her Lord
    And takes her labour up.

1882.

LXII. . . . . C. M. P.

And there shall be night no more; and they need no light of lamp, neither light of sun.—Rev. xxii. 5.

I.

O LAND of day, eternal day,
    Unbroken by a night:
No need of candle nor of sun
Thy blessed fields to shine upon,—
    The Lamb of God thy light.

II.

O land of life that cannot die,
    To mortals open'd up:
No more the drooping of the eye,
The parting word, the fitful sigh,
    The bitter-tasting cup.

III.

O land of rest and sweet content,
    The time of battle o'er,

The weary victors, laying down
The cross, receive from Christ the crown
   To wear forevermore.

IV.

O land of beauty, beautiful
   Beyond the brightest dream
Of poet in his time of power:
No painter in his happiest hour
   Has caught its faintest gleam.

V.

Lord of the land! Eternal King
   Of a domain so fair!
O give us grace to watch and wait,
On duty at the outer gate,
   Till we may enter there.

1877.

LXIII. . . . . 7, 6, P.

Amen: Blessing, and glory, and wisdom, and thanksgiving, and honour, and power, and might, be unto our God for ever and ever.—Rev. vii. 12.

I.

GLORY be to God on high!
   Glory in the highest!
Lord of wondrous majesty,
Maker of the earth and sky:
Saints redeem'd and angels cry,
   Glory be to God on high!
   Glory in the highest!

II.

Glory be to God on high!
   Glory in the highest!
Father, Son, and Holy Ghost!
Praises in the uttermost
Earth shall sing with heaven's host:
   Glory be to God on high!
   Glory in the highest!

1883.

LXIV..... 8, 8, 8.

Why seek ye him that liveth among the dead? He is not here, but is risen.—Luke xxiv. 5, 6.

I.

CHRIST is risen! O the wonder!
Rending bands of death asunder,
Rising to the glory yonder!

II.

Silently as morning breaking
Came the wonderful awaking,
Christ again his Godhead taking:

III.

In the stillness of the morning,
Angels heralding no warning,
Though the world's new light was dawning.

IV.

Ere sunrising, one came seeking,
She whose heart with pain was reeking,
Tears her pallid cheek bestreaking.

V.

Last she saw him faint and dying;
Stark and cold her Lord was lying,
Ere she left him, weeping, sighing.

VI.

Lone she stood in tearful wonder:
Who had rent His tomb asunder?
Who so vile the grave to plunder?

VII.

She, amazed, her watch was keeping,
Blinding mists her vision steeping:
"Woman, why art thou a-weeping?"

VIII.

Was the startled woman chary?
Was she in her answering wary?
What a change when He said, "Mary!"

IX.

Once the piteous supplication,
Now the glad ejaculation,
"Master!" in rapt adoration.

X.

No more mocking, no more scourging,
Priest and mob the soldiers urging,
While the rage of hell was surging:

XI.

Crown of thorns no longer wearing,
Cruel taunts no longer bearing,
Nails no more his body tearing:

XII.

Majesty and gracious sweetness
Join in him with perfect meetness,
God and man in full completeness.

XIII.

Lord Jehovah! low before thee,
Ransom'd by thee, we adore thee:
Glory in the highest! Glory!

1882.

LXV. . . . . DIES IRÆ.

An attempt (based mainly on a literal rendering by J. Addison Campbell) to give in English verse the famous Latin hymn of Thomas of Celano, written in the thirteenth century.

I.

THE day of wrath, that certain day,
In glowing embers earth shall lay,
Both David and the Sybil say.

II.

With trembling dread the world will quake
Or e'er the Judge shall inquest make,
And ruin all things overtake.

III.

The trump shall sound a startling tone
Throughout the graves of every zone,
And call all men before the throne.

IV.

And death and nature in surprise
Shall see the creature man arise
To answer at the dread assize.

V.

The written book will forth be brought,
With good and evil records fraught,
And man be judged for deed and thought.

VI.

When he shall sit upon his throne,
The Judge will make all secrets known;
Things unavenged there shall be none.

VII.

And what shall wretched I then plead?
Who then for me will intercede,
When e'en the just will mercy need?

VIII.

King of tremendous majesty,
Who sav'st thine own by grace most free,
Thou fount of pity, rescue me!

IX.

Remember, Jesus kind, I pray,
For me thou gav'st thy life away:
Then do not lose me on that day!

X.

While seeking me, I wearied thee;
Thou on the cross redeemedst me:
In vain let not such travail be!

XI.

Just and avenging Judge, I cry,
Give me remission ere I die,
Before the reckoning-day comes nigh.

XII.

A culprit groaning with his care,
My face the blush for sin shall wear;
O God, the pleading suppliant spare!

XIII.

The Magdalene was forgiven,
And e'en the thief by thee was shriven;
Thou giv'st me also hope of heaven.

XIV.

My prayers, unworthy, do not spurn;
Thou who art good, in kindness turn,
Lest I in fire eternal burn.

XV.

Far from the goats' accursèd band
Keep me apart, and make me stand
Among the sheep at thy right hand.

XVI.

When the accursed go to their place,
When dies the furious flame apace,
Then call my name with words of grace.

XVII.

Prostrate and suppliant, I pray,
With spirit crush'd to ashes gray,
O care for me at my last day!

Upon that day of tearful eyes,
When from the embers he shall rise,
And culprit man wait thy decree,
O God, then pardon even me.

    Kind Lord Jesus, ever blest!
    Give to thy redeeméd rest.

                    Amen.

1882.

LXVI. .... 8, 7, 4.

A man had two sons; and he came to the first, and said, Son, go work to-day in the vineyard.—Matt. xxi. 28.

I.

IN the vineyard of our Father
   Daily work we find to do;
Scatter'd fruit our hands may gather,
     Though we are but weak and few:
       Little clusters
   Help to fill the basket too.

II.

Toiling early in the morning,
   Catching moments through the day,
Nothing small or lowly scorning,—
     So we work, and watch, and pray;
       Gathering gladly
   Free-will offerings by the way.

III.

Not for selfish praise or glory,
    Not for objects nothing worth,
But to send the blessed story
    Of the gospel o'er the earth,
        Telling mortals
    Of our Lord and Saviour's birth.

IV.

Up and ever at our calling,
    Till in death our lips are dumb,
Or till—sin's dominion falling—
    Christ shall in his kingdom come,
        And his children
    Reach their everlasting home.

V.

Steadfast, then, in our endeavour,
    Heavenly Father, may we be:
And forever, and forever,
    We will give the praise to thee;
        Alleluiah!
    Singing, all eternity.

1845.

LXVII. . . . . 7, 6.

The morning stars sang together, and all the sons of God shouted for joy.—Job xxxviii. 7.

I.

THE morning stars were singing
　With joy when time began;
And heavenly peals were ringing
　When God created man:
The universe was swelling
　With jubilant delight,
While all to all were telling
　The Lord Jehovah's might.

II.

A higher song of glory
　Was sung in after-days,—
And shepherds heard the story,
　As angels hymn'd His praise,—
Of Jesus in a manger,
　God's well-belovéd Son,
Who came to save from danger
　A race by sin undone.

III.

A multitude of voices
    Have learn'd this holy song;
And earth with heaven rejoices
    To roll the sound along.
With saints and angels o'er us,
    Singing before the throne,
We join the gladsome chorus,
    Glory to God alone!

1846.

LXVIII. .... 8, 7, 4.

Wilt thou not from this time cry unto me, My Father, thou art the guide of my youth?—Jer. iii. 4.

I.

Father! in my life's young morning,
   May thy word direct my way:
Let me heed each gracious warning,
    Lest my feet should go astray:
      Make me willing
    All its precepts to obey.

II.

Father! gentle is thy teaching;
   Be a docile spirit mine:
Every day thy grace beseeching,
    Let thy loving-kindness shine
      Always on me,
    And my heart be wholly thine.

III.

Father! let me never covet
    Things of vanity and pride:
Teach me truth, and may I love it
    Better than all else beside:
        Blessed Bible!
    May it be my heavenward guide.

1841.

LXIX. . . . . 7, 6.

Giving thanks always for all things.—Eph. v. 20.

I.

I THANK the Lord my Maker
    For all his gifts to me:
For making me partaker
    Of bounties rich and free:
For father and for mother,
    Who give me clothes and food,
For sister and for brother,
    And all the kind and good.

II.

I thank the Lord my Saviour
    Who came for me to die,
And bless me with his favour
    And fit me for the sky,—
That, all my sins out-blotted,
    By Jesus wash'd away,
I may be found unspotted
    When comes the final day.

III.

I thank the Lord for giving
　　The Spirit of his grace,
That I may serve him living,
　　And, dying, reach the place
Where Jesus in his glory
　　I shall forever see,
And tell the wondrous story
　　Of all his love for me.

1844.

LXX. .... H. M.

Thou makest the outgoings of the morning and evening to rejoice. Thou visitest the earth, and waterest it: thou greatly enrichest it with the river of God.—Ps. lxv. 8, 9.

I.

WHO bids the wind to blow?
    Who makes the sun to shine,
And flowers and grass to grow
    Around this path of mine?
Who makes these shady trees arise,
And spread their boughs beneath the skies?

II.

Who makes this brook, so bright,
    From earth's cold bosom spring,
And sparkle in the light,
    And sweetly, sweetly sing,
As if an angel lent his voice
To help the rippling stream rejoice?

III.

Who gave the airy bird
    Soft feathers and swift wings,
And taught it music-words
    To charm us when it sings?—
Say, little bird! who taught you how
To sing so sweetly on that bough?

IV.

O, 'tis our Father, God,
    Who gives us every thing:
The grass, the flowery sod,
    The brook, and birds that sing;
And all the blessings of this day
He sheds upon our happy way.

V.

How good is God! He gave
    His only Son to die,
Our souls from death to save,
    And fit us for the sky.
O, let us bow, and serve him here
With gratitude and love sincere.

1842.

LXXI. .... 8, 7, 8, 4.

Thy word is a lamp unto my feet, and a light unto my path.
Ps. cxix. 105.

I.

BOOK of grace, and book of glory!
  Gift of God to age and youth;
Wondrous is thy sacred story,
  Bright, bright with truth.

II.

Book of love! in accents tender,
  Speaking unto such as we;
May it lead us, Lord, to render
  All, all to thee.

III.

Book of hope! the spirit sighing
  Consolation finds in thee,
As it hears the Saviour crying,
  "Come, come to me."

IV.

Book of peace! when nights of sorrow
    Fall upon us drearily,
Thou wilt bring a shining morrow,
    Full, full of thee.

V.

Book of life! when we, reposing,
    Bid farewell to friends we love,
Give us for the life then closing,
    Life, life above.

1843.

LXXII. . . . . 6, 9.

"At the Beautiful Gate of the Temple."—Acts iii. 10.

I.

THERE is light on my path,
　　There is joy in my heart,
For the doubt and the fear
　　From my bosom depart,
While I muse on his love
　　As I quietly wait
For the Master to come
　　At the Beautiful Gate,
The Beautiful Gate of the temple.

II.

There is travailing care;
　　There is labour in vain;
There is noise in the air;
　　There is pitiless rain;

And I cover my head
    Till the storm shall abate,
And the Lord shall appear
    At the Beautiful Gate,
The Beautiful Gate of the temple.

III.

I am sorely beset;
    I am weary and worn;
And I sigh for the night,
    And I long for the morn:
He will come in good time,
    Whether early or late,
As I kneel for his touch
    At the Beautiful Gate,
The Beautiful Gate of the temple.

IV.

Lo! the darkness is past,
    And the morning is here;
'Tis the voice of my Lord
    That enraptures my ear:
He has come to my help
    In my uttermost strait,
And he beckons me in
    At the Beautiful Gate,
The Beautiful Gate of his temple.

1885.

LXXIII. . . . . 8, 9.

"Ye know not when."—Mark xiii. 35.

I.

I KNOW not when the Lord will call,
    Or in the night or in the morning:
The angel's foot may softly fall,
    Or it may give a note of warning.

II.

There may be but a step between
    Earth's outer gate and heaven's portal:
Or morn may slowly lift the screen
    That hangs before the day immortal.

III.

The Lord may whisper, "Follow me!"
    When none but I shall hear the calling,
And men may marvel when they see
    A tree in summer greenness falling.

IV.

Perchance I may be left to wait,
  His earlier-chosen taken only,
And I may feel 'tis getting late,
  And earth is growing dim and lonely.

V.

Perchance when gladsome days are come,
  Or when the wintry winds are blowing,
The Lord will bid me hasten home,
  Unquestioning and all unknowing.

VI.

The time, the way, I'd leave to Thee:
  Were mine the choice, this would I rather,
Content that both alike shall be
  As seemeth best to thee, my Father.

1885.

LXXIV..... L. M.

"Whom God hath hedged in."—Job iii. 23.

I.

THE sea before, the foe behind,
What place of hiding can I find?
Shut up from help on every side,
What hand my trembling feet will guide?

II.

From Satan's realm I sought to flee,
And now behold the raging sea!
The foe is pressing on me sore,
And I shall perish on the shore.

III.

When I set out to 'scape his sway
The guide-posts pointed me this way:
Is there no arm this side the wave
The hunted fugitive to save?

IV.

The treacherous deep my soul may snare,
And yet away far over there
The haven of salvation lies,
Its borders reaching to the skies.

V.

And must I venture in the sea?
Is there no other path for me?
Will the same hand that led me here
For my deliverance now appear?

VI.

O Lord, my Saviour! hear my cry:
In my distressful day come nigh:
Now, trembling, on the waves I tread,
O hold me in this time of dread.

VII.

The waters part before my feet;
Onward I press with footsteps fleet:
Dry-shod I reach the farther strand
And enter in Immanuel's land!

VIII.

Forevermore Thy praise I'll sing:
Glory to thee, Eternal King!
'Tis thine to order all my way,
Be mine unquestioning to obey.

1885.

LXXV. . . . . 7's.

"Draw nigh unto my soul."—Ps. lxix. 18.

I.

NEARER to thy heart of love;
  Nearer to thy hand of power:
  Jesus! nearer every hour
Lift me to the life above.

II.

Nearer unto thee, my Lord,
  Who art always near to me,
  Though thy hand I may not see
As it guides me heavenward.

III.

Nearer to thy gracious throne
  May thy Spirit draw my feet,
  Nearer to thy mercy-seat,
Seeing none but thee alone.

IV.

Nearer when the morn shall break,
 Nearer when the sun goes down,
 Let thy loving-kindness crown
All the way my feet should take.

V.

Nearer in the crowded day,
 Nearer in the secret place,
 Let the sense of present grace
In my peaceful bosom stay.

VI.

Nearer when my trembling hand
 Lifts the dreaded cross with fear,
 Though I shed the human tear
When, bereft, I mutely stand.

VII.

Nearer, Jesus, to thy breast
 As my daily need is more,
 Till thou openest the door
Leading to the heavenly rest.

1885.

LXXVI. .... 7, 6.

"O my soul, why art thou disquieted within me?"—Ps. xlii. 11.

I.

My soul! why sit forsaken
    In sorrow's darken'd tent?
Why should thy trust be shaken
    By griefs thy Lord hath sent?

II.

It was the love he bore thee
    That led him to the cross:
That love is ever o'er thee,
    To save thee, soul, from loss.

III.

Go, climb faith's sacred mountain,
    Unweighted by thy fears;
Arise above the fountain
    That feeds the stream of tears;

IV.

And thou shalt see far over
    The mist that dims thine eyes,
And then shalt thou discover
    The bow across the skies.

V.

It is not always raining;
    It is not always night:
His grace shall shame thy plaining;
    Thy God is always right.

VI.

In lovingness he reigneth
    O'er all his family,
And whatso he ordaineth
    Is ever best to be.

VII.

Then let thy night of sadness
    Bring in the grateful day,
And thou shalt walk in gladness
    With Jesus by the way.

1885.

LXXVII. .... C. M.

"Look unto me, and be ye saved."—Isaiah xlv. 22.

I.

'TIS but a looking unto Christ
    In penitence and trust,
And he bestows the grace unpriced
    That counts the sinner just.

II.

'Tis but a doing of his will,
    The work of faith in love,
And he the passing days shall fill
    With blessings dream'd not of.

III.

'Tis but the leaving in his hands
    The morrow with its cares,
And peace within the bosom stands
    An angel unawares.

IV.

'Tis but a word of comfort said,
    A simple, kindly deed,—
Yet 'tis a precious ointment shed
    Upon a soul in need.

V.

'Tis but the bearing patiently
    The wrongful word, the sneer,
And love shall turn the enmity
    Of hate's empoison'd spear.

VI.

'Tis but a look of tenderness
    On weepers left behind
That lingers evermore to bless
    The sad and lonely mind.

VII.

'Tis but the closing of the eye,
    The ceasing of the breath,
Then comes the hour of victory,
    The triumph over death.

VIII.

'Tis but a lifting of the latch
    That fastens glory's door,

And wondrous sights the eye shall catch
   On heaven's resplendent floor.

IX.

'Twas but an erring child of earth
   With mortal sandals shod:
Lo! now, of an immortal birth,
   He lives with Christ in God.

1885.

LXXVIII. . . . 8, 4.

"Hold thou me up, and I shall be safe."—Ps. cxix. 117.

I.

BUILD up, O Lord, a rampart-wall
    Along my way,
That, journeying onward, I withal
    Go not astray.

II.

Whene'er the road be rough and steep,
    And I, foot-sore,
Over the rocks but slowly creep,
    Give strength the more.

III.

When noon shall pour upon my brow
    Its burning heat,
Beside the shadowing rock guide Thou
    My faltering feet.

IV.

While walking lonely in the dark,
    No hand in mine,
Vouchsafe a star, a heavenly spark,
    On me to shine.

V.

When lost amid a tangled wild
    Of fear and doubt,
Good Shepherd, seek the erring child
    And lead him out.

VI.

The fruit of earth's forbidden trees
    Let me not taste;
Nor lag, nor lie in bowers of ease,
    When I should haste.

VII.

If e'er I meet one overborne
    Or faint of heart,
May I, instead of careless scorn,
    Good cheer impart.

VIII.

Let me not loiter on the edge
    Of any sin,
Lest, dallying on the slippery ledge,
    My feet slide in.

IX.

Yet, if unheedingly they slide,
    Thy grace I crave:
Be thou my rescuer and guide;
    Lord Jesus, save!

X.

When I come near, all worn and scarr'd,
    Thy mansions blest,
Then, Saviour, let me find unbarr'd
    The gate of rest.

XI.

Among the multitudes that throng
    The holy place,
Be mine to sing in loving song
    Thy sovereign grace.

1885.

LXXIX. . . . S. M.

"*For thy great mercies, O Lord, hear.*"—Dan. ix. 18, 19.

I.

O FATHER, for thy love!
    O Saviour, for thy grace!
O Comforter, as heaven above
    Be this thy dwelling-place.

II.

O for the promised gift!
    O for the gracious rain!
Let not thy church, O Lord, uplift
    Her hungering prayers in vain.

III.

O for the touch of power!
    O for the tongues of flame!
O for the coming of the hour
    To glorify thy name.

IV.

O for the tender heart!
O for the loving fear!
Blest Holy One, the gift impart
   Thy still, small voice to hear.

V.

Hasten the rising sun!
O drive away the night!
Soon may thy sovereign will be done,
   Thy kingdom come in might.

1885.

LXXX. . . . . 8, 7.

"Yet he bare the sin of many."—Isa. liii. 12.

I.

O THE darkness, O the sorrow,
   O the misery of sin!
When will dawn the promised morrow
   That shall bring deliverance in?

II.

One there was ordain'd to languish,
   Guiltless, in Gethsemane:
One there was who died in anguish,
   Innocent, on Calvary.

III.

Jesus was the burden-bearer,
   God's own Son the sacrifice,—
Of the griefs of man the sharer,
   Of his soul the ransom-price.

IV.

'Tis the Christ, the ever-living,
    Ever-loving, ever-blest,
By the Comforter still giving
    Pardon, holiness, and rest.

V.

Can the love so freely given,
    Can the blood so freely shed,
Fail to draw the earth to heaven,—
    Fail to bring alive its dead?

VI.

Rise, O children of the Father!
    Stand, ye brothers of the Son,
In unyielding ranks together
    Till the crown of Christ be won:

VII.

Till the lands of sin and sorrow,
    Darker than the ancient night,
Shall behold the promised morrow
    Beam on them with saving light.

1886.

LXXXI. . . . . 8, 9.

"Caught up into Paradise."—2 Cor. xii. 4.

I.

BEFORE the silver cord be loosed,
   Or e'er the golden bowl be broken,
   By Christ's redeem'd is heard and spoken
A language ne'er by earthlings used.

II.

While waiting for his call of grace,
   The links of life as yet unriven,
   A new-created sense is given
That pierces the immeasured space.

III.

The spirit, newly clothed upon,
   Out-reaches to the gates eternal,
   And glimpses of the realms supernal
Eclipse awhile the natural sun.

IV.

So Stephen saw the Son of man
   At God's right hand enthroned in glory,
   And while with martyr-baptism gory
His life on high with Christ began.

V.

And so, through time's on-speeding years,
   Some ripening saints, with favour gifted,
   Anear God's presence have been lifted
While dwelling in these lower spheres.

VI.

Of old, the shepherds saw on high
   His angels in their bright apparel,
   And heard redemption's wondrous carol,
Alone, beneath the midnight sky.

VII.

If distant glories of the throne
   Transfigure now our earthly mansions,
   What powers, what insights, what expansions,
When we shall know as we are known!

1886.

LXXXII. . . . 8, 8.

"Thou makest the outgoings of the morning and evening to sing."
Ps. lxv. 8.

I.

DAY is waning into shadow;
　Darkness dims the hill and meadow,
Till the stars light up the even
As they climb the hills of heaven.

II.

With its lantern earthward swinging,
See the firefly heavenward winging;
While from crannied wall and thicket
Comes the carol of the cricket.

III.

Peace, with hushing finger lifted,
Cheers the heart by sorrow rifted,
Pointing to the Comfort-Giver
And the home beyond the river.

IV.

As an island ocean-bounded,
Lord, thy love hath me surrounded,—
Love in sunlight, love in showers,
Bringing precious fruits and flowers.

V.

Thou hast given from thy treasure
Bounties more than I can measure:
Yea, my Father! not a minute
But has come with goodness in it.

VI.

Years there were that brought me crosses;
Times of pain and grief and losses;
Still they carried in their keeping
Sowing-time and harvest-reaping.

VII.

As the span of life shall lengthen,
Lord, my faith and patience strengthen:
Daily to thee bring me nearer,
Daily to me be thou dearer.

VIII.

After thine, O holy Saviour!
Pattern'd be my life's behaviour:
Less of self in all my bearing,
More for others daily caring.

IX.

When shall come the soul's undressing,
May I fall asleep with blessing,
And await thy call of waking
When the heavenly day is breaking.

X.

Past all earthly joy and weeping,
What a waking after sleeping,
When the new-born eye beholdeth
What thy grace, dear Lord, unfoldeth!

1886.

LXXXIII. . . . . 8, 7.

To them that love God all things work together for good.
Rom. viii. 28.

I.

COLD the bed and hard the pillow,
    Yet the wanderer slept near heaven:
Wild the wind and high the billow,
    Yet the bark was homeward driven.

II.

Bitter were the tears of sorrow,
    Yet the drops were turn'd to balm:
Darkly loom'd the dreaded morrow,
    Yet it broke in heavenly calm.

III.

Fiery darts above him flying,
    Yet beneath faith's shield he lay:
Weary paths before him lying,
    Yet a brook was by the way.

IV.

Heavy seem'd the cross unlifted,
 Yet 'twas light when taken up:
Empty was the rock unrifted,
 Yet a blessing fill'd the cup.

V.

Fierce the furnace sevenfold heated,
 Yet the Son of God was there:
By the evil ill-entreated,
 Yet the Lord his sorrow bare.

VI.

Often worn and heavy-laden,
 Yet there came a perfect rest
When the soul, his promise stay'd on,
 In the Lord was ever blest.

1887.

LXXXIV. .... 8, 8, 8.

God, who giveth us richly all things to enjoy.—1 Tim. vi. 17.

I.

FATHER! all is of thy giving:
All of good from thee receiving,
This the wherefore man is living:

II.

This the blessedness of being,
Led by thee, the One All-seeing,
In the ways of thy decreeing.

III.

By the power of thy Spirit,
Only in thy dear Son's merit,
Daily grace do we inherit.

IV.

On our upward journey going
In the strength of thy bestowing,
Building up or overthrowing:

V.

Overthrowing things of meanness,
In their prime or budding greenness,
Pride and passion and uncleanness:

VI.

Evil thought and evil speaking,
Words with hate and envy reeking,
Grasping greed and selfish seeking.

VII.

Building not of wood and stubble
Things that perish like a bubble
In the day of fiery trouble:

VIII.

But of gold and gems the rarest;
Stones the strongest and the fairest;
Earnest deeds for which thou carest:

IX.

Precious gems of love undying;
Patient, faithful, self-denying;
Sturdy stones that stand the trying.

X.

Not for honours transitory,
Not for name in passing story,
But to thy most sovereign glory.

XI.

Nor of our own wisdom, Master!
Else we work alone disaster:
Lord! be thou our life's forecaster.

XII.

This thy children's joy in living,
Kingly gifts from thee receiving,
Love and service to thee giving.

1888.

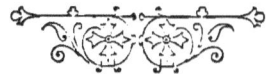

LXXXV. . . . . S. M.

Let him sit alone, and keep silence, because He hath laid it upon him.
Lam. iii. 28.

I.

BE still, my soul! be still,
   Nor hide thee in the cleft;
But to thy Father's loving will
   Be thy deliverance left.

II.

But little dost thou know,
   But little canst thou see
Of the unfoldings of the plan
   That grasps eternity:

III.

That holds the child of days,
   That holds the angelic throng,
And spans the countless worlds that move
   Their starry path along.

IV.

Yet God will not forget
    The ransom'd of his grace:
The gift of his belovéd Son
    Doth every gift embrace.

V.

His mercy hovers round
    Thy pathway every hour:
His loving-kindness is as vast
    As his almighty power.

VI.

Be quieted, my soul!
    In sweet content abide:
If night be long, the day will come,
    And thou'lt be satisfied.

VII.

My soul! bless now the Lord,
    Thy hope, thy rock, thy King!
Thy Father, Saviour, Comforter,
    E'en in the darkness sing.

1889.

LXXXVI. .... 8, 7.

I will meditate also upon all thy work, and muse on thy doings.
Psalm lxxvii. 12.

I.

SITTING in the twilight musing
    On the days that come and go,
Joys and sorrows, interfusing,
    Mingled in a sunset glow:
All were of the Father's choosing,
    Gifts most fitting to bestow.

II.

Often had the sun been shining:
    Yet e'en when the day was chill,
Shower and sunshine, intertwining,
    Rainbows flung from vale to hill,
And the soul, its self resigning,
    In the peace of God lay still.

III.

When, the Saviour's voice unheeding,
    In the depths the spirit lies,

We see not the ladder leading
    Upward to the holy skies,
Till the Hand for us once bleeding
    Touch with sight our blinded eyes.

IV.

Evermore the Shepherd careth
    For the gather'd of his fold:
Still the wandering ones he beareth
    From the darkness and the cold:
Still he healeth, still he spareth,
    As on earth he did of old.

V.

O what love and pity bideth
    In the bosom of our Lord!
He that in His truth confideth
    Finds the treasure in it stored,
That for him His grace provideth
    An exceeding great reward.

VI.

Musing in the quiet chamber
    Of the soul at eventide,
If we stir some ashy ember
    Of a fire that long had died,
Penitent, may we remember
    Christ our Lord was crucified!

1889.

Psalms.

FOURTH PSALM.

L. M.

My righteous God! O hear my call:
    For thou, of old, didst not forbear
Deliverance in my sore distress;
    O pity me, and hear my prayer.

Ye sons of man! how long will ye
    Pervert my glory into shame,—
Ye that love falsehood, seeking lies,
    To bring dishonour on my name?

But know, Jehovah for himself
    Hath set his chosen ones apart;
And when I call on him, he hears
    The cry that rises from my heart.

O rage no more, and cease from sin:
    Communing with your heart, be still:
Right sacrifices offer up,
    And trust ye in Jehovah's will.

The many say, "O that we might
    The time of good and plenty see!"
Lift thou, O Lord! on us the light
    Of thine own presence graciously.

Thou hast put gladness in my heart,
    More than they have from corn and wine:
In peace will I lie down and sleep,
    Thou, Lord, alone preservest thine.

1889.

FIFTH PSALM.

VERSES 1-3, 7, 8, 11, 12.

C. M.

GIVE ear unto my words, O Lord!
    And heed my yearning sigh:
My King, my God! O hear my voice,
    For unto thee I cry.

And in the morning, thou, O Lord,
    Shalt hear my voice arise:
At dawn will I set forth my prayer,
    And wait with watching eyes.

Through thy great loving-kindness, in
    Thy house will I appear,
And toward thy holy temple, Lord,
    Will worship in thy fear.

Lord, guide me in thy righteousness,
    So foes may rage in vain;
And make thy way before my face
    Lie open as a plain.

Let them be glad and shout for joy
    That refuge take in thee:
Defend thou them that love thy name,
    And let them joyful be.

Unto the righteous man, O Lord,
    Thy blessings e'er abound:
With favour dost thou compass him
    As with a shield around.

1889.

EIGHTH PSALM.

C. M.

O LORD, our Lord! in all the earth
    Thy name how excellent!
O let thy glory be inscribed
    Above the firmament!

Out of the mouth of very babes
    And sucklings dost thou build
A tower of strength by which the wrath
    Of vengeful foes is still'd.

When I behold thy heavens, O Lord,
    Thy finger-work divine,—
The moon and stars which thou hast set
    In their high place to shine,—

What is a mortal man, that him
    Thou in thy mind shouldst bear?
Or what a son of Adam's race,
    That thou for him shouldst care?

But little lower made than God,
    With fear and glory crown'd,
Dominion hast thou given to him
    Over thy works around;

Under his feet the creatures placed,
    The flocks and herds, yea all;
And on the wild beasts of the field
    His fear is made to fall:

The airy birds, the restless fish
    That through the waters sweep,
And whatsoever glideth through
    The pathways of the deep.

O Lord, our Lord! in all the earth
    Thy word of power didst frame,
How excellent the glory is
    Of thine eternal name!

NINETEENTH PSALM.

7, 6.

THE heavens declare the glory
    Of their creator God;
The firmament revealeth
    His handiwork abroad.

Day unto day outpoureth
    Its speech in silent praise,
And night to night is breathing
    The knowledge of his ways.

Though speech be not, nor language,—
    Their voice none comprehend,—
Through earth their power extendeth,
    Their words go to its end.

A tent far in the heavens
    He setteth for the sun,
And there his rest he taketh
    What time the day is done.

He like a bridegroom steppeth
    Forth from his resting-place,
And boundeth like a warrior
    Again to run his race.

From heaven's extreme he speedeth
    Its circuit to complete;
And there is nothing hidden
    From his resistless heat.

Jehovah's law is perfect,
    The soul it rectifies;
And true his testimony,
    The simple making wise.

Right are Jehovah's precepts;
    They cause the heart to sing;
And clear is his commandment,
    The eyes enlightening.

His fear-compelling glory
    Forever shall endure;
And righteous are his statutes,
    Their truthfulness is sure:

Than gold more to be sought for,
    Fine gold that mines entomb,

And sweeter than the honey
    That droppeth from the comb.

Thy servant is instructed
    By them, most gracious Lord,
And in the keeping of them
    There is a great reward.

So high thy law, so holy,
    Who, of himself, can learn,
With all his inner searching,
    His errors to discern?

From faults unconscious clear me,
    And make me pure within;
Keep back thy servant also
    From all presumptuous sin.

Let it not have dominion,
    Then blameless I shall be,
And from the great transgression
    Thy grace shall hold me free.

My Rock and my Redeemer!
    Before thee be each word
And each heart-whisper'd musing
    Acceptable, O Lord.

1887.

FORTY-SIXTH PSALM.

7, 6.

A REFUGE and a fortress,
    Our God is on our side,
A very present helper
    When trouble doth betide.

Therefore, though earth be shaken,
    Our souls will never fear,
Though in the heart of oceans
    The mountains disappear.

What though the troubled waters
    In roaring foam shall break,
And their tumultuous swelling
    Shall make the mountains quake:
      The Lord of hosts is with us,
        Our refuge and our strength.

There is a heavenly river
    Whose streams shall never dry,
That gladdeneth God's city,
    The place of the Most High.

God in the midst of Zion
    Is evermore her stay;
Her he will help right early,
    E'en at the dawn of day.

The nations roar'd, the kingdoms
    Were riven to their base,
And when his voice he utter'd
    The earth did melt apace.
        The Lord of hosts is with us,
            Our refuge and our strength.

Behold Jehovah's doings,
    What wonders he hath wrought,
What awe-pervading silence
    On earth his hand hath brought.

The wars among the nations
    His word compels to cease,
And earth to all its borders
    He quieteth with peace.

The warrior's bow he shivers,
    The spear asunder rends;
The chariots he burneth
    Amid the fire he sends.

Be still; and know, ye nations,
    That I am God alone,
And I will be exalted
    O'er every land and throne.

The Lord of hosts is with us,
    The God of Jacob is
Our refuge and our fortress:
    Be glory alway his!

1888.

SIXTY-SECOND PSALM.

C. M.

ONLY in silence wait on God:
    My soul! thy help is He;
My rock, salvation, and defence,
    Unshaken I shall be.

How long will ye assail a man
    And hunt him as a prey,
Till he become a tottering wall,
    A fence that giveth way?

Their only thought to thrust him down,
    In lies is their delight:
While blessing with the mouth, their heart
    Doth curse with hidden spite.

Only in silence wait, my soul!
    My hope in God alone,
My rock, salvation, and high tower,
    I shall not be o'erthrown.

My glory and my help is God,
    My safeguard from all harm;
My refuge and my rock of strength
    Is his almighty arm.

O put your trust in him alway,
    Ye people who are his:
Pour out your heart before your God,
    For he our refuge is.

Only a breath are men; the sons
    Of nobly-born a lie;
For in the balance they go up,
    A breath of vanity.

Trust not in wrong, nor vainly boast
    The crafty spoiler's art;
And if your riches grow apace,
    On them set not your heart.

One thing hath God himself declared,—
    Yea, two things have I heard,—
That power belongeth unto God!
    Yet grace is in this word;

For loving-kindness, Lord, is thine,
    While justice rules thy thought;
Thou renderest to every man
    As he his work hath wrought.

1888.

NINETY-SEVENTH PSALM.

L. M.

JEHOVAH reigns! Let earth rejoice;
    And let the multitude of isles
Be glad, and sing with tuneful voice,
    And nature's face be clad in smiles.

Though clouds and darkness from afar
    Are round about his presence known,
Yet righteousness and judgment are
    The habitation of his throne.

A fire before him goes, and burns
    His enemies on every side;
His lightnings flash; and earth by turns
    Beholds and trembles in its pride.

The hills before his presence melt,
    Like wax before the furious flame;
His presence by the earth is felt
    Who built her everlasting frame.

The heavens declare his righteousness,
    The people all his glory see;
While they who serve the images,
    And boast in them, confounded be.

Then Zion heard, and she was glad;
    The daughters of Judea sang
Rejoicingly, and through the land
    The praises of thy judgments rang.

For thou, O Lord! above the earth
    Art high; thou art exalted far
Above the kings of mortal birth,
    Though lofty their aspirings are.

Hate evil, ye that love the Lord,
    For he preserves the saintly soul;
And every danger he will ward,
    And save from wicked men's control.

On righteous men shall light arise,
    Like morning breaking o'er the hills;
And hope shall kindle in their eyes,
    While holy mirth their bosom fills

Rejoice, ye righteous, in the Lord!
    Give thanks before his presence now;
In memory of his faithful word
    And holiness, give thanks, and bow.

1853.

ONE HUNDRED AND TWENTY-FIRST PSALM.

6's.

I LIFT my longing eyes
   Up to the hills in vain:
Whence shall my help arise
   In time of want and pain?

My help is from the Lord
   Who gave all creatures birth,
And by his forming word
   Created heaven and earth.

No lurking enemy
   Thy foot shall turn astray,
For he that keepeth thee
   Will slumber not for aye.

Behold, he who in love
   Doth Israel ever keep,
His watchfulness shall prove,
   And slumber not nor sleep.

Thy keeper is the Lord,
    Jehovah is thy shade
On thy right hand: his word
    Thy sure defence is made.

By day the fervid sun
    Thy head shall never smite,
Nor shall the sickly moon
    Assail thee in the night.

Preserving thee from harm,
    All evil he'll control;
And his most gracious arm
    Shall e'er preserve thy soul.

When thou dost outward go,
    His grace shall go before;
In coming in also,
    Now and forevermore.

1871.

ONE HUNDRED AND FORTY-FIFTH PSALM.

C. M.

I WILL extol thee every day,
    My God, O glorious King;
And I will bless thy name for aye,
    Thy praise forever sing.

Great is the Lord and wonderful,
    And greatly to be praised:
His greatness is unsearchable,
    Beyond the heavens raised.

One generation, praising thee,
    Shall testimony bear
Unto the next, and wonderingly
    Thy mighty acts declare.

The honour of thy majesty,
    Thy wonders I'll proclaim;
Thine acts of terror men shall see
    And glorify thy name.

The memory of thy goodness they
    Shall utter far and wide;
Thy righteousness from day to day
    Shall sing on every side.

The Lord is gracious; full of kind
    Compassion: he is slow
To anger, and his holy mind
    Is great in mercy too.

The Lord our God is good to all,
    For all are in his thought;
His tender mercies richly fall
    On all that he hath wrought.

Thy works shall praise thee evermore,
    And thee thy saints shall bless;
Thy kingdom's glory and thy power
    To all the world confess; .

Thy mighty acts that all may know
    Among the sons of men,
Thy kingdom's majesty to show
    To every creature's ken.

An everlasting kingdom's thine,
    And thy dominion sure

Throughout all generations' time
    Shall everywhere endure.

The Lord upholdeth all that fall,
    The bow'd with sorrow riven;
While on thee wait the eyes of all,
    Their meat is duly given.

Thou openest thy hand of grace,
    And thou dost satisfy
The wants of all in every place
    Who for thy presence cry.

The Lord is righteous in his ways,
    His works are holy all:
He's nigh to those that love his praise,
    And on him truly call.

The strong desire he will fulfil
    Of them that fear his name:
He hears their cry, and he will still
    Save them from harm and shame.

The Lord preserveth them from harm
    Who love him as their joy,
But wicked men his wrathful arm
    Will utterly destroy.

My mouth shall joyfully proclaim
   His praise from day to day:
Let all flesh bless his holy name
   Forever and for aye.

871.

DOXOLOGIES.

L. M.

ALL praise to Thee, the trinal One,
The Holy Father, Holy Son,
And Holy Spirit! Thou alone
Art King on the eternal throne.

C. M.

O HOLY, holy, holy Lord,
The Father and the Son
And Holy Ghost! Be thou adored
While endless ages run.

S. M.

BESIDE Thee there is none:
Eternal God and King,
The Father, Son, and Holy Ghost,
Thy glorious praise we sing.

7, 6.

THY love, O Holy Father,
    Thy grace, O Holy Son,
Thy peace, O Holy Spirit,
    Thy church abide upon:
While she her voice upraises
    To thine eternal throne,
And chants in endless praises
    Glory to God alone.

8, 7.

GLORY be to God the Father:
    Halleluiah!
  Glory be to God the Son,
    Halleluiah!
And to God the Holy Spirit,
    Halleluiah!
  In eternal being one!
    Halleluiah!
May his kingdom come in power;
    Halleluiah!
  And his holy will be done:
    Halleluiah!
  Halleluiah in the highest!
  Halleluiah evermore!

7's.

GLORY to Thee evermore!
Glory in the uttermost!
Heaven and earth thy name adore,
Father, Son, and Holy Ghost.

8, 7, 4.

GLORY in the highest! glory!
Father, Son, and Holy Ghost:
King eternal! we adore thee,
Singing with the heavenly host,
Glory! glory!
Glory be to God on high!

Finis.

www.ingramcontent.com/pod-product-compliance
Lightning Source LLC
Chambersburg PA
CBHW020824230426
43666CB00007B/1094

promisit et manucepit fideliter premissa omnia per nos sibi injuncta facere et adimplere sub poena predicta et ad hec dedit nobis fidejussores dictum comitem de Sutherland, Alexandrum de Moravia Dominum de Culbyn et Thomam de Chisholme.

Registrum Moraviense, p. 353, No. 271.

END OF VOL. I.

Printed by R. Clark, Edinburgh.

APPENDIX No. XXVII.

EUFAMIA, SEVENTH COUNTESS OF ROSS.

JUDGMENT pronounced by ALEXANDER, Bishop of Moray, and ALEXANDER, Bishop of Ross, on the differences between ALEXANDER STEWART, Earl of Buchan, and EUFAMIA, Countess of Ross, his spouse—1389.

CHRISTI nomine invocato . Nos Alexander et Alexander Moraviensis et Rossensis ecclesiarum Episcopi Dyocesani partium subscriptarum judicesque ordinari sedentes pro tribunali de peritorum consilio quibus hec omnia communicavimus auditis que utraque pars contra aliam proponere voluit pronunciamus . . . et declaramus in his scriptis Dominam Eufamiam Comitissam Rossie restituendam esse Domino Alexandro Seneschallo comiti Buchanie et Domino de Ross tanquam viro suo et marito una cum possessionibus suis et quantum de jure possumus restituimus tractandam maritali affectione honeste in lecto et in mensa . in victu . . . secundum decenciam sui status Mariotamque filiam Athyn amovendam fore et quantum de jure possumus amovemus et quod ipse eam de cetro non dimittat et quia Domina Eufamia allegat timorem mortis et hominum suorum nativorum nobilium dictus comes manucapiet nobis et securitatem fidejusariam magnarum et notabilium personarum et sub poena ducentarum librarum nobis inveniet quod ipsam tractabit in omnibus honeste ut supra dicitur et sine periculo mortis et hominess suos nativos nobiles et alios contra jus commune in aliquo non artabit In quarum testimonium sigilla nostra sunt appensa Lecta lata et in his scriptis pronunciata fuit hec nostra sentenia in ecclesia fratrum predicatorum de Inverness . . 2 Novembris 1389, presentibus magnifico viro Roberto Comite de Sutherland Ada Abbate de Kynloss et multis aliis testibus ad premissa vocatis Qui quidem Alexander ibidem personaliter constitutus

Appendix XXVII.

1389.

1389.